HELEN OF THE GLEN

HELEN OF THE GLEN

A Story of Christian Heroism

Adapted by

George F. MacLean

Illustrated by Catherine Miller Ellis

Christian Focus Publications

Published by
Christian Focus Publications
Houston, Texas, U.S.A.   Tain, Ross-shire, Scotland

©1988 Christian Focus Publications
ISBN 0 906 731 80 1

CONTENTS

Preface... 7

Chapter 1   Wrathburn's Wrath.................. 9

Chapter 2   Helen's Vow..........................13

Chapter 3   Off To The Big City................17

Chapter 4   Tortured...............................21

Chapter 5   Near To Death......................25

Chapter 6   Taken To Task......................29

Chapter 7   Devastating News...................33

Chapter 8   Life And Death.....................37

Chapter 9   A Changed Man....................41

Glossary..45

PREFACE

*'They lived unknown
till persecution dragged them into fame
and chased them up to heaven'.*

Cowper

This is an exciting story. We are told about the life and struggle for her Christian faith of a young girl in dangerous times. Originally written by Robert Pollock (1798 — 1824). George F. MacLean has presented this story in a fresh lively way which ensures that you will want to finish it.

Helen's witness to her family and others is a fine example for us.

W.H.M.M. 1988

HELEN OF THE GLEN

CHAPTER ONE

WRATHBURN'S WRATH

One hand clutching a well worn Bible and at the same time gathering up her long skirt so that she could run quickly, Mrs Thomson held tightly to her frightened seven year old daughter. Her heart raced. Her lungs gasped for breath. Her legs felt like jelly.

'Come awa', ma little one. Dinna' stop. Keep gaen', urged Mrs Thomson.

Yet her own body called out for her to stop and fear alone sustained her headlong flight. Behind her she could hear the shouts of soldiers.

'It's yur bluid we're aifter and nothin' less, ye la' braiker!'

These coarse voices thundered threats of terror which chilled her blood. As the drum of hooves and the jingle and slap of harness grew louder her heart filled with a dread which drove from her mind all thought of her aching muscles and heaving chest.

What wrong had she done? What was her monstrous crime? Mrs Thomson's crime was to worship God at a secret open air service (or conventicle). These conventicles had been banned by the government over three hundred years ago. Those who held these secret services were called Covenanters. They believed that Scotland had a duty to uphold the Presbyterian church and to resist the government's attempts to interfere with the church. A great number of the important people in Scotland had at one time signed a covenant which was a kind of promise to God. Some had even signed it using their own blood instead of ink to show how strongly they felt. The kings of those days were no friends to the Presbyterian church and bitterly opposed the Covenanters and many of Mrs Thomson's country men and women suffered in what was known as 'the killing times'. The fate of those who refused to compromise flashed before Mrs Thomson's mind as she dashed from her home. Mrs Thomson stayed at Cleughead in a remote glen in Ayrshire, near Loudon Hill.

Less than a mile away from their home Mrs Thomson and her daughter Helen were overtaken. Foam-flecked horses careered wildly onto the road before them and reared as they were heavily reined in. Sabres were pointed at Mrs Thomson and Helen and Mrs Thomson was roughly seized by the soldiers. Their commander was notorious. Duncan Wrathburn was no officer and gentleman. He was a ruthless ruffian. He took sadistic pleasure in hounding and persecuting the Covenanters. Torture and murder were his stock in trade and made him universally feared and detested.

'Wuman', he barked, glaring fiercely at her and pointing his musket at her, 'tak' the Test or tak' the shot in ma musket'.

The Test was a promise to give up attending conventicles, to accept the complete power of the king in church affairs and to reject the idea of covenants with God.

Mrs Thomson fell on bended knees.

'Sir', she pleaded, 'dinna' force me tae gang against ma conscience.'

Wrathburn was well named. Swearing terribly, he commanded her to take the Test or he would blow her brains out.

Terrified as she was, Mrs Thomson was made of stern stuff. Her faith was strong and her loyalty to Christ unswerving. She knew whom she believed in and what she believed. To her, God's love was more than life.

'I canna' and willna' forsake ma faith or ma God. But I'm just a poor widow, sir. Spare me. Ma husband died fighting fur his king an' country. Think o' ma young dochter here — and hur younger brither. Fur their sake dinna' shoot me.'

Wrathburn was unmoved by her pleas.

'Nane o' yer whinin', wuman. Say yur prayers, an' dinna' tak' ou'r lang. Ye've nae mair than a meenit left.'

Her eyes lining with tears, Mrs Thomson turned to her daughter.

'Helen', she said, 'they are gaen tae kill me, an' ye an' William will be left as helpless orphans. But God will be yur Faither. Niver forsake God an' He will niver forsake ye. Helen, teach yur little brither aboot Christ so that we will a' meet at last in Heaven.'

'Cut it short', cried out Wrathburn.

Mrs Thomson commended her soul to Christ and Wrathburn took aim. Helen screamed.

'Sir do ye nae think....'

'Had yur wheesht, ye insubordinate saftie!' roared Wrathburn.

The roar was echoed by the bang of the musket as he shot Helen's mother through the heart.

'Hur bluid be on hur ain heid!' he cried, and galloped off.

CHAPTER TWO

HELEN'S VOW

The Sabbath stillness had been shattered by the musket shot. Not far distant, a shepherd had been startled and alarmed. He worked for the farmer on whose land stood Mrs Thomson's thatched cottage. Whit could the loud bang hae been? There wis nae thunder and naebody hunted on the Sabbath and there had been a scream. The conventicle! That wis it. Sojers had broken up the service and were at thir deathly business.

Warily but speedily he made his way in the direction of the bang. What a dreadful sight met his eyes: Little Helen clinging to her dead mother and weeping with great gasping sobs. The mother's blood soaked her daughter's dress. He comforted Helen as best as he could and led her to the farmhouse. Mrs Thomson had left Helen's little brother there. Only five years of age, he had been too small to go to the service. As he entered the farmhouse kitchen Helen's sobbing broke out afresh. The farmer's wife, clattered the pan she was holding, down onto the old range and bustled over.

'Whit's wrang? Whit's wrang?' she said anxiously.

'It's the dragoons. They broke up the conventicle. Puir Helen's mither wis shot doon wi' nae mercy. Ah heard the shot an' came across Helen greetin' her een oot an' lyin' ou'r her mither's body.'

'The black-hairted brutes! Sojers? They're nae sojers. They're the de'il's bairns. Puir wee Helen. Ma hert bleeds fur ye.'

In came the farmer. He too was shocked and outraged by the brutality and heartlessness of the murder.

'Whit can we say tae William? How can ye tell a five-year old?'

The pain of telling William and their sense of horror that such a good woman should have been shot before her daughter like a dog were to haunt the farmer and his wife till their dying hours.

As soon as he could recover his wits and see that Helen and William were looked after, the farmer organised some men and went to fetch Mrs Thomson's body into the farmhouse.

Two days later Mrs Thomson was buried near the spot where she had been killed. The farmer led the simple service. The few mourners felt their hearts bleed for the pathetic, tearful orphans, but in Helen's mind a strong resolve was being formed. Her mother's last words to her had been imprinted on her memory:

'Niver forsake God an' He will niver forsake ye. Helen, teach yur little brither aboot Christ so that we will a' meet at last in Heaven.'

As she stood holding her brother's hand at the graveside she vowed to herself:

'This is gaen tae be ma Kirk. Ah'm gaen tae read ma Bible here, Ah'm gaen tae pray here an' ah'm gaen tae repeat tae William oor maw's last words.'

Shortly after the funeral, a smooth granite stone was laid flat on Mrs Thomson's grave and her name was engraved on it. In the coming years Helen and William sat on that gravestone countless times. There Helen prayed with William, taught him about God and told him all she could remember about her mother. Her vow at the funeral service was faithfully kept and that spot was a treasured and holy spot for her.

The plight of Helen and William would have been dreadful had it not been for the farmer, Mr George Paton. He took Helen and William into his farmhouse and cared for them like a father. Once he had been the shepherd employed by Mrs Thomson's father. When Mrs Thomson's parents and relatives had fallen on hard times, he had obtained the farm. Because of the connection with her family he had welcomed Mrs Thomson and given her the use of the thatched cottage when her husband's business in Glasgow had failed. Her husband had felt obliged to join the army in order to support his wife and family. He had died overseas while in the army. The farmer who had treated Mrs Thomson kindly now willingly looked after her orphaned children. He was a God-fearing man, with a tender heart.

The farmer's family didn't find it hard to accept Helen and William. They felt really sorry for them and, anyway, Helen and William were clever and likeable. A farmhouse is a busy place and Helen could sew and knit. There wasn't a school nearby so Helen and the farmer's wife saw to it that William was taught to read. As they grew up, William became useful in herding the cows and Helen helped in the dairy.

CHAPTER THREE

OFF TO THE BIG CITY

What excitement Helen and William felt at having an important visitor, especially when their visitor had come all the way from Glasgow. Even the farmer's occasional visitors who only came from the farms round about were not half as grand. See how splendid his clothes were, how well tailored and expensive. The gentleman was called Mr Hunter. He had been a friend of their father when their father had been in business in Glasgow.

When they were taken in to see Mr Hunter their excitement was replaced with shyness. But soon they were goggle-eyed and full of questions as Mr Hunter described the wonders of Glasgow: The Clyde where ships plied back and forth, the bustle and noise of the streets, the magnificent buildings, the splendid houses of the merchants and the goods sold in the shops. Mr Hunter could fairly talk. William especially was fascinated.

Mr Hunter could see William's eyes sparkle. A shrewd man, he could see that William was an eager, clever lad.

'William', he said, 'how would you like to come to Glasgow and work for my firm? You'll get a good training and you could do well for yourself, my boy.'

William was speechless with amazement and delight. He could scarcely believe his ears.

'Do ye really mean that, Mr Hunter?'

'Of course I do, William. It's a great opportunity you know.'

'Ah know that, Mr Hunter. I'd love tae gang wi' ye, ah really would. Thank ye, Mr Hunter. This is incredible. But whit about ye, Helen?'

'Mr Hunter is a very respectable man, Helen,' interposed the farmer. 'Ye couldna' get a mair honest person. If he taks William under his wing he'll came tae nae hairm.'

'Ah'll miss ye, William', said Helen, 'but if ye promise tae remember whit oor mither's last words were and tae read yur Bible an' pray, I'm happy tae see ye fixed wi' a guid job. We canna' thank ye enough, Mr Hunter.'

It was an autumn morning when William, not yet twelve, and Mr Hunter set off. Helen was fifteen. She and the farmer accompanied William and Mr Hunter for a mile or two. When it came to the time to part, the farmer warned William of the dangers and the temptations in Glasgow.

'Ye ken, William, that there are mony temptations an' pitfa's in Glesga?'

'Ah ken that, Mr Paton.'

'Well, it's nae every lad that has enough sense tae keep tae the straight an' narrow. Remember that temptations come frae the de'il an' help comes frae God. The de'il loves darkness an' if ye read yur Bible that will be a lamp tae yur feet and a licht tae yur path.'

'Aye, Mr Paton. Ah'll nae forget.'

Then Helen reminded him of their mother's parting words, 'Niver forsake God an' He will niver forsake ye'.

Then they hugged and said goodbye to each other. William and Mr Hunter set off over the moors to Glasgow.

William was not disappointed with Mr Hunter's description of Glasgow. It was new and strange and exciting. There were dark crowded tenements and fine Churches. There were smoky workshops and rattling carriages. The Clyde flowed majestically through the city and the distant hills gathered clouds. Commerce flourished, and so did crime. The city throbbed with life. Despite being so young and despite being a country boy, he did not feel at all homesick. Being eager to learn, he quickly settled down and adapted to his work. He was taught writing, accounts and business practice. Mr Hunter was very pleased with his progress.

William remembered, too, the advice given to him by Helen and the farmer. His companions were godless and they laughed at him for keeping the Lord's Day. Nevertheless he read the Bible, and despite his companions' mockery, he still prayed and attended Church faithfully.

But as time passed he became more attracted to the carefree ways of his friends. They seemed so smart when they swaggered and boasted. They were so lively, so sociable. Gradually he became more forgetful of the good habits of his life at Cleughead. Despite occasional pangs of conscience he became more and more careless.

CHAPTER FOUR

TORTURED

Helen steeled herself. The farmer had fled to a secret hiding place at word that the soldiers were coming. It was well known that he attended the conventicles and that his house was a haven for persecuted Christians. Helen had stayed in the dairy. If they found her, that would delay the soldiers and give the farmer time to hide. He was growing old.

Calling out gruffly and uttering dire threats, the soldiers burst into the dairy. Wrathburn, mercifully, was not among them. His arm had been nearly severed in a battle with Covenanters who had taken up arms to defend themselves.

'Whit dae ye want?' asked Helen as calmly as she could.

'That fox o' a fairmer, of course. Whit lair is Paton hidin' in?' rasped the officer.

'Why dae ye want tae ken?' asked Helen. She was stalling for time.

The officer was not amused. His face went purple and with a vicious kick he sent a milk pail flying.

'Tae deal wi' a rebellious pious fraud an' teach ye fanatical Covenanting scum a lesson. Noo answer me. Whaur is he?'

'I willna' tell ye. He's an auld man. He's like a faither tae me.'

She looked the officer straight in the face. The next moment a stinging blow sent her crashing to the straw covered floor. Rough hands hauled her to her feet.

'We'll mak' ye talk, a' richt. Get the matches ready.'

Helen gazed aghast as the soldiers struck flints and lit the tinder. The matches were lit. The officer grabbed her hair and yanked her head back.

His face, only inches from hers, he hissed, 'Whaur is he? Tell us an' ye'll come tae nae hairm.'

Helen said not a word.

'Ye'll be sorry', snarled the officer. 'Let's hear ye scream.'

The men drew nearer. Helen flinched. Desperately she prayed for grace to endure the agony. Her fingers were forced apart. She shut her eyes tightly as the burning matches were placed between her fingers. She yelled in pain. The matches were taken away.

'Noo, talk', snapped the officer.

Helen sobbed but didn't say a word.

'Again!'

The pain was searing and intense. She screwed up her eyes and clenched her teeth. She was determined not to scream.

Several times the soldiers tortured her in this way and not a word did they wring from Helen's lips.

Foiled, baffled and furious, the officer drew his sword. Helen thought her end had come. He swung his sword and struck her neck with the flat of his sword.

'Curse yur obstinacy', he yelled. 'But dinna' think that'll

save him. He will hang by his thumbs frae the raifters o' his ain barn.'

As they clattered out of the farm yard Helen was able, despite the pain where her fingers had the flesh burned to the bone, to express to God her thankfulness for the grace given to her to stay faithful. The farmer was safe.

CHAPTER FIVE

NEAR TO DEATH

While Helen was suffering in the persecution William was pursuing his career in Glasgow. Because of these troubled, dangerous times William was not able to visit his sister. However, the persecution made the Stuart line of kings very unpopular. In what became known as the Glorious Bloodless Revolution Prince William of Orange was invited to become king and James II of England fled. Peace and Presbyterianism were restored in Scotland.

Over three years had passed, therefore, before William was able to visit Helen and the old farmer. It was a clear, crisp, frosty morning in January when he passed through the suburbs of Glasgow. Eleven miles south of Glasgow he rested on the summit of Ballageich Hill and admired the view. Then he set off across the moors. Loudon Hill was near Cleughead and he used that as his landmark.

After the long hours at an office desk and the routine of city life, he was really enjoying his tramp across the moors. In this buoyant mood he failed to notice the change in the weather. Before he was properly aware of it, the sky was grey and heavy and an ominous heaviness filled the air. Then an occasional flake of snow fell. The wind started to rise and within minutes the moor was engulfed in a furious blizzard.

The fierce wind whipped the snowflakes into his face and stung his eyes. All visibility was blotted out. He struggled against the driving snow and staggered through peat bogs.

He could see nothing but swirling snowflakes and hear nothing but the howling of the wind.

In danger of falling into bogs, totally without sense of direction in the featureless white-out and choked up with the snow, he stood still. He remembered how he had misused the Lord's Day, forgotten to read his Bible and neglected prayer. He pictured in his mind Helen's earnest face as she reminded him of their mother's advice. Would he ever see Helen again? Like others before and after him, he prayed desperately that God would rescue him. Oh how he promised that if he were spared he would never again forget God! Though the storm gradually abated, darkness fell and a keen frost chilled him to the marrow. Numb, lost, totally exhausted and overwhelmed with despair, he sank to the ground.

His prayer, however, had been heard. Out of the gloom a sheepdog emerged. It sniffed and whined at the semi-conscious figure before bounding off into the snow. Soon it was back with its master. William was lifted up and given some warm milk to revive him. His arm round the shepherd's shoulder, William stumbled through the snow. A mile away they reached shelter. William was never so thankful to see the light of an oil lamp at a window. The old man of the house was a true Christian. He washed William's feet, warmed a bed for him and prepared a hot meal. William slept the sleep of an utterly exhausted man.

He awoke with a start. Whit was that loud groan? He felt a hand on his arm. It was the old man of the house who had been sitting beside William's bed.

'There's nae cause tae be alarmed. Just tak' it easy. There's an old sojer in that bed ou'r yonder. He arrived here twa or three days ago utterly worn oot an' in bad shape. He's got a high fever an' tosses an' turns an' groans. He used tae be well kent an' feared. He's called Wrathburn. He wis a hertless monster in his day. He's the one wha shot doon the widow o' Cleughead .... Hey, whit's wrang?'

William was dumbfounded. Wrathburn! His mother's killer!

'I — I canna' believe it. Do ye ken wha ah am? It was ma mither that Wrathburn shot!'

It was the old man's turn to be dumbfounded.

'Ah — ah'm sorry tae hear that. This must be terrible for ye.'

'Dinna' tell him wha ah am, will ye?'

'Nae, of course not. When he gets delirious he often mentions the widow o' Cleughead. It preys on his mind. He's is tormented by guilt and doom. His mind is filled wi' fear o' hell. I've tried tae speak to him o' God's mercy but that jist seems tae mak' him rant an' rave a' the mair.'

William shuddered. Later on he got up and moved closer to Wrathburn's bed. The dying wretch looked appalling. His cheek bones protruded. His glazed, sunken eyes gazed ahead. His breath came in gasps. A rotten stump or two of teeth could be seen in his half open mouth. His grey beard was dirty and untrimmed. Every now and then he would groan, shout out hoarsely, try to prop himself up and collapse, gasping feebly. Terror was in his eyes and his haverings were a mixture of curses, recollections of his atrocities and talk of hell.

Later that day Wrathburn breathed his last. This fearful end had cast a gloom over the house. Despite the kindness he had received, William was glad to leave the house after another night's rest. The memory of the horrible, godless, hopeless death of Wrathburn was nightmarish.

CHAPTER SIX

TAKEN TO TASK

What a welcome William received! In three years he had shot up and had lost his boyish look. Helen hugged him and stood back to admire his fashionable clothes and handsome appearance. As far as she knew she had every cause to be proud of him.

'Noo, William', said the old farmer when the first wave of excitement had receded, 'tell us aboot Glesga an' yur work there'.

William was glad to oblige and Helen and the farmer were well entertained with vivid descriptions and amusing stories.

'Noo ye must be tired, William', said Helen at length. 'Ye'll need some food. Whit kind o' journey did ye hae?'

William's face grew serious.

'It's a miracle ah'm here. If it wisnae fur a shepherd's dog ah'd hae been dead on the moors a couple o' nichts back, I wis caught in a dreadfu' blizzard.'

'Oh, puir William!' exclaimed Helen.

'Then a very strange thing happened. In the hoose I was taken tae ah met a man I'd niver thocht ah'd ever see.'

'Wha wis that?' asked Helen.

'Wrathburn.'

'Wrathburn!' exclaimed Helen, totally taken aback.

'Yes, Wrathburn.'

William told them the whole unhappy story. Wrathburn's manner of death deeply distressed Helen. She was a sensitive girl.

It was at sunset the next day when Helen and William visited their mother's grave. Most of the day had been very wet. The evening star had made its appearance as they reached the spot, accompanied by a pet lamb which Helen had hand reared. William could scarcely make out his mother's name in the fading light. The evening hush, the growing darkness and the memory of all the visits they had made to that spot all combined to bring a lump into William's throat.

As she always did, Helen prayed and then reminded William of their mother's words, 'Niver forsake God an' He will niver forsake ye'.

It was several days before Helen detected that William's attitude to spiritual matters had become lukewarm. She was alarmed to find him thinking that one could be a Christian and yet act in the same way as the men of the world.

'Some o' ma friends pay nae heed tae religion yet they seem tae get on fine. They micht mak' fun o' the Bible occasionally, but they're o'richt really, and they're a' well liked', argued William.

'People micht hae a high enough opinion o' them, but is that whit really matters? Surely it's whit God thinks o' them that's important', countered Helen.

'But God kens that we're only flesh an' bluid. We've a' got oor faults but God's merciful an' forgiving, Helen. He willna' hold minor flaws an' blemishes agin us.'

'William, I'm surprised at ye. Ye oucht tae ken better than that. It is tae the sinner wha repents that God promises forgiveness an' mercy, nae tae the careless people o' this world wha dinna' care a button fur God or their ain souls.'

Helen knew her Bible and marshalled her arguments well. The Christian, she argued, cannot serve two masters. According to Psalm One the man God blesses does not walk in the counsel of the ungodly, or stand in the way of sinners or sit in the seat of the scornful, God promises that whatever he does shall prosper.

William could not answer her arguments or resist her sincerity. He promised not to pay attention to his companion's views any more.

It was with Helen's advice fresh in his mind that William set out on his return journey. When he returned to Glasgow his promises to Helen, his narrow escape from death on the moors and the awful death of Wrathburn all made him pay far more heed to spiritual matters than before.

Alas, all William's Bible reading and prayers were the result of a merely human resolve. He had not been born again of the Spirit of God and therefore had no spiritual strength. After a while he started to perform these religious duties hastily. Then they became irregular and at last virtually non-existent. Outwardly he was respectable. He still attended church. But among his wordly companions he would joke about religion and take God's name in vain. He was far more concerned with business success than being right with God. His social life and his career prospered, but spiritually he was impoverished.

William was extremely fond of Helen, despite his forgetfulness of her warnings and her example. He wrote her frequently. His plan was that once he had done well for himself in business he would take Helen to Glasgow where she would keep house for him. He imagined that the society and fashions of Glasgow would soften Helen's views. Despite being only seventeen, William had already been given a share in the business by Mr Hunter so he could look forward to having his sister by his side, well provided for and dressed elegantly in the style of the day. Almost daily he dreamed of their happiness together in a grand and spacious merchant's house.

CHAPTER SEVEN

DEVASTATING NEWS

It was a lovely May afternoon over two years since William's first visit to his sister. William was strolling along a Glasgow street with one of his friends, soaking in the sunshine and admiring the beauty of the day.

He noticed a lad coming in the opposite direction and dressed in the typical clothes of a country boy. Country boys were very often teased and tormented by the city dwellers. They were called names and mocked. Practical jokes were played on them. William was always ready to help any young lad from the country new to Glasgow. He had once been in that bewildering situation himself. The lad was looking at the signs and numbers on the houses.

As William went up to the country boy, he was astonished to see that it was Mr Paton's nephew. He worked for his uncle, the farmer, as a shepherd boy.

'Whit are ye doing here?' William gasped.

'Oh, Mr Thomson, ah'm glad I've found ye. Glesga is sic a big place an ah got lost several times. Ah wis looking fur ye. Ah'm afraid I've got bad news. Helen is ill.'

'Ill? Whit's wrang wi' hur? How bad is she?' demanded William.

'She caucht a very severe cold some months ago. She niver recovered frae it an' has got worse recently. She's confined tae bed noo an' very weak. The doctor disnae think she 'll get ou'r it.'

William was stunned. This disturbing news had shattered his dreams. His first impulse was to dash off to Cleughead.

'We'll hae tae hurry', he urged. 'Ah'll need tae get a Glesga doctor tae gang.'

'There's nae use setting off today', said the shepherd lad. 'By the time ye get a doctor the day will be wearin' on. Ye dinna' want tae be stuck oot on the moor in the dark.'

'Ye're richt. I just wisnae thinkin'. We'll set off at first licht in the morn.'

After quizzing the shepherd lad to get a more detailed picture of Helen's state of health, William told Mr Hunter of his sister's illness, arranged for a good doctor to go to Cleughead the next morning and took the shepherd lad to his own lodgings.

Again he fretted about Helen.

'Why did she nae send for me afore noo?'

The shepherd boy did not answer and averted his eyes.

'Whit's wrang? Are ye hiding something frae me? Has Helen heard something aboot me?'

The shepherd boy nodded reluctantly.

'She heard that ye were mair concerned aboot yur worldly career than aboot yur spiritual welfare. She became desperate tae see ye an' told me tae bring ye tae see hur as quickly as ah could.'

'Wha told her that?' asked William, his heart heavy.

'A travelling merchant wha kens ye', replied the boy. 'She just couldna' rest aifter she heard that.'

William was up early the next morning, but that night was the longest in his life. No longer was his mind crammed with thoughts of business deals or of plans for future wealth or of anticipated worldly pleasures in the company of his friends. As he tossed and turned his thoughts were of Helen, of the possibility of her recovery and of the worry and alarm he had caused her. That was bound to sap her strength further and hasten the progress of her illness. How his cherished hopes of bringing her to Glasgow had been dealt a mortal blow! He remembered how they had wandered together in their native glen as children and how they had visited their mother's grave. Especially the sweetness of Helen's voice whispered in his ear as he recalled her repeating to him their mother's dying advice.

At first light of day William and a doctor were mounted on horseback and ready for the road. Among their provisions were medicines which might possibly help Helen. Their journey was over rough terrain but the fine May weather had dried up the bogs. The raging torrents produced by winter storms and melting snows had shrunk to gurgling streams which were easily forded. Not stopping for any refreshments, they pressed on urgently. At ten o'clock that day an anxious William, his heart racing, entered Helen's house at Cleughead.

CHAPTER EIGHT

LIFE AND DEATH

William went alone to his sister's room. The turmoil in his heart was almost unbearable — a fearful hoping against hope struggled with a dismal pessimism. Anxiety about his sister was mingled with self-reproach and guilt at the distress he had caused her.

Helen lay propped up in bed. One look at her complexion and her hollow face withered every hope William had of her recovery. He needed no medical expertise to tell that medical expertise was of no help now.

Helen raised herself up. William leaned over her. She put her arms around him and kissed him. She shrugged off his anxious questions about her health. All she was concerned about was him. Bitter regret for his neglect of all she had urged him to remember stabbed his heart. He groaned inwardly but his agony of conscience was obvious in his face. Insinctively Helen knew that this was no pious pretence. William was heartfelt and sincere. She relaxed.

'Helen, ah've brocht a doctor wi' me frae Glesga. Will ah bring him in?'

'That wis really kind o' ye, William, but I dinna' think he can do me ony guid.'

William brought the doctor in to see Helen in any case. What William had realised immediately was no less obvious to the doctor: The case was hopeless. Although she was in no pain Helen was very weak and growing weaker and weaker. As gently as he could the doctor gave William his opinion. It was unnecessary. William's own verdict on Helen had already been confirmed by the look on the doctor's face. The doctor promised to stay till the next day to find out more about Helen's condition. The servant girl might be able to give more information which would help him with his diagnosis.

William went out into the garden and threw himself down beneath an old hawthorn tree in bitterness of soul. What memories flooded into his mind! — his visits to his mother's grave with Helen, his narrow deliverance from death in the raging blizzard and the fearful death of the doomed Wrathburn. His witty, swaggering companions in Glasgow — they were giddy asses. He himself had been one of them. Helen was pure gold and he was dross. How his heart had deceived him! How dark had been his spiritual state! How carelessly he had lived!

As the wretchedness of his spiritual condition was burned into his consciousness, there dawned on his soul a new awareness of the meaning of Christ's death. As he cried for mercy, he saw the mercy of God in Christ not as a part of Christian teaching merely to be accepted but as something he desperately needed. Precious indeed was the blood of Jesus which alone could cleanse him from his guilt. All Helen's teaching and advice flashed across his mind and he blessed God for her and how she had been the means used to bring the light and grace of God into his soul. After praying for Helen, he returned to her room.

He found their faithful friend, the old farmer, with Helen. He had been talking with her about her hope of eternal life. The farmer left them to themselves. William told her about what had happened in his soul, while he was in the garden — about his spiritual struggle and deliverance. Radiant with joy, Helen clasped his neck and kissed him. But even as she spoke of how she was content to die now and to be with Jesus, her hands slipped from his neck. She had breathed her last. The emotion of the moment had been too much for Helen.

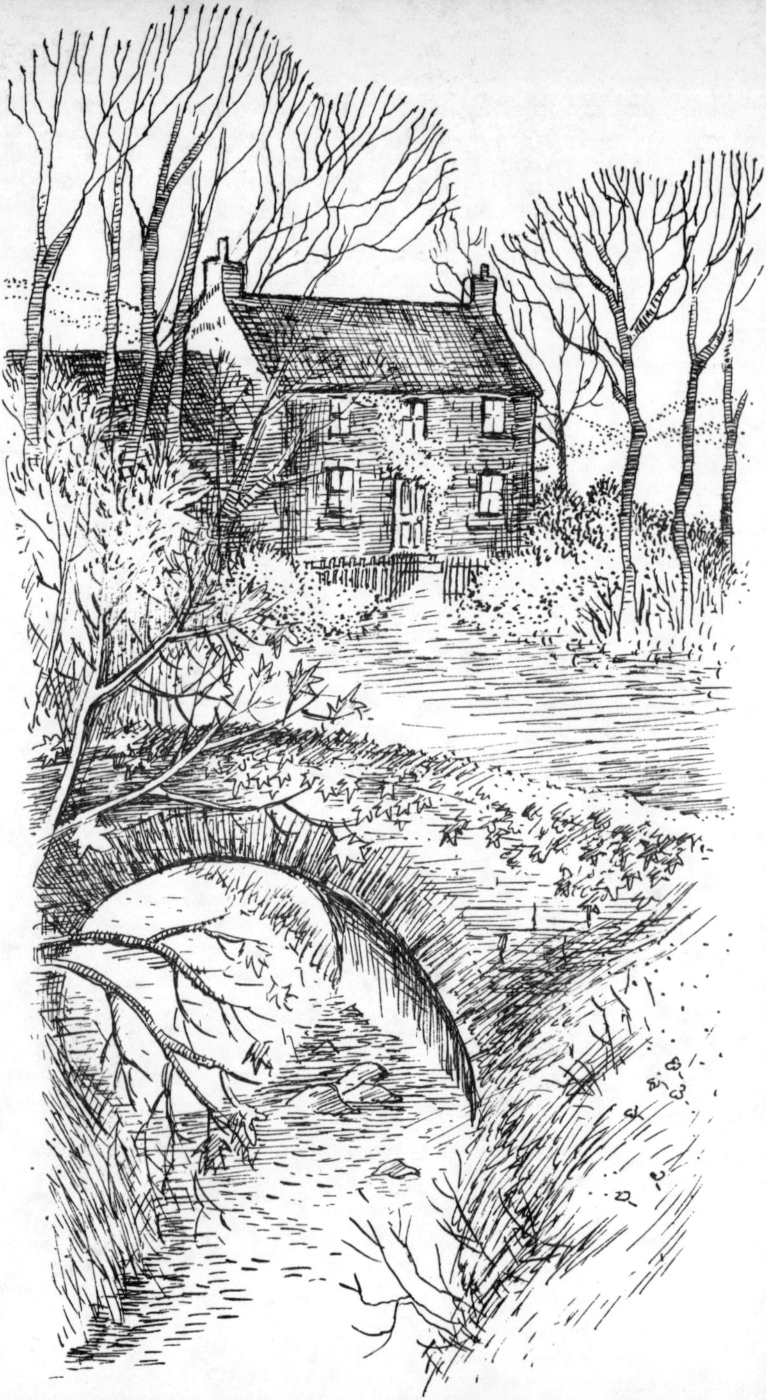

CHAPTER NINE

A CHANGED MAN

Two days later Helen's funeral procession moved with dignified slowness to the village graveyard about five miles distant. Helen had always been tender hearted and had loved animals, so no-one had the heart to turn away her pet lamb (no longer a lamb) from following the procession. The chief mourners included the old farmer and his nephew, the shepherd boy. The old farmer had known the suffering of Mrs Thomson and Helen and had seen both mother and daughter buried.

After the funeral William arranged for a stone to be erected over Helen's grave, with his sister's name engraved on it, along with these words of Jesus: 'Weep not for me, but weep for yourselves.' Helen, he believed, had gone to a better place where there are no more tears.

It was a changed man who returned to Glasgow. His companions did not like the change. They put up with it at first as they thought it was due to the temporary effects of grief. It was soon obvious that the change was deep and permanent. Soon, too, they were accusing him of religious mania.

'Look, man', they said, 'all this religious nonsense is daft. Your reason is being blinded by religious delusions. If you don't watch it you'll go crazy.'

But this did not shake his resolve to follow Christ wholeheartedly.

'We're all having a get together tonight. We'll all have a rare old time. There's no need to go over the score or get drunk. It's just some harmless fun. Don't be an old sobersides.'

'Ah'm sorry, but ah canna' gang wi' ye. Ye see, ah've lost all interest in these things. My joy is found in Jesus. Ah'd far rather be wi' God's people in God's house.'

He had to reckon with loss of popularity and with jibes and ridicule. His former friends with whom he had joked about the Bible now argued with him and tried to prove that the Bible was false. The ridicule was borne patiently, but William knew how to reply to irreverent attacks on scripture, urging his godless companions to examine their lives in the light of God's Word. There they would see themselves as if in a mirror. Attack is sometimes the best method of defence. William pointed out how illogical and hypocritical they were. They accused him of narrowness of outlook yet their own narrowness was abundantly evident. They were intolerant of his faith. They were not content to accept his new way of life. They mocked his beliefs. Some William impressed with his witness and stand for what he believed. Others turned their backs on him. But as he grew in stature as a Christian he became the kind of man whom even the scoffers had to respect, even if they did so grudgingly.

William never married, he never forgot the sister who was the cause of the great and lasting change in his spiritual history. At the advanced age of ninety-five the old shepherd died. His nephew, the shepherd boy, fell heir to the farm. He had married the servant who had looked after Helen in her illness. It was to their home, then, that

William returned every summer. Every year he spent a week or two with them and visited the graves of his mother and Helen.

At the end of his days it was from that same house, the one he had been brought up in when he had been orphaned, that his body was carried to its resting place in that glen that had witnessed the tragic but beautiful and holy life of the girl who came to be known as Helen of the Glen.

GLOSSARY

aboot — about
afore — before
ah — I
ah've — I've
aifter — after
ain — own
an' — and
auld — old
awa' — away
bairns — children
black-hairted — blackhearted
bluid — blood
braiker — breaker
brither — brother
brocht — brought
canna' — cannot
caucht — caught
couldna' — couldn't
dinna' — don't
disnae — doesn't
dochter — daughter
doon — down
de'il — devil
dae — do
dreadfu' — dreadful
een — eyes

fairmer — farmer
faither — father
frae — from
fur — for
gaen — going
gang — go
Glesga — Glasgow
greetin' — crying
guid — good
had yur wheesht — be quiet
hae — have
hairm — harm
heid — head
hert — heart
hertless — heartless
hidin' — hiding
hoose — house
hur — her
is — as
jist — just
ken — know
kent — known
Kirk — church

GLOSSARY

la' — law
lang — long
licht — light
lyin' — lying
ma — my
mair — more
mak' — make
maw — mum
meenit — minute
micht — might
mither — mother
mony — many
nae — no
naebody — nobody
nane — none
nichts — nights
niver — never
noo — now
nothin' — nothing
o' — of
ony — any
oor — our
oot — out
ou'r — over
oucht — ought
pitfa's — pitfalls

puir — poor
raifters — rafters
richt — right
saftie — softie
sic — such
sojers — soldiers
tae — to
tak' — take
thir — their
thocht — thought
twa — two
wee — small
wha — who
whaur — where
whit — what
whinin' — whining
wi' — with
willna' — will not
wis — was
wisnae — wasn't
wrang — wrong
wuman — woman
ye — you
yur — your

Also published by
CHRISTIAN FOCUS PUBLICATIONS

Seek and Find

Are you looking for children's stories? SEEK AND FIND has sixteen, plus illustrations and quizzes

This sequel to CHILDREN'S CHOICE skilfully uses everyday situations to illustrate Bible truths and lead children to Jesus.

Carine Mackenzie, author of SEEK AND FIND, has also written:

CHILDREN'S CHOICE
THE TWO MARGARETS
THE NAMES OF JESUS
PEOPLE JESUS MET
and
Eleven Bibletime Books

The Puzzling Book

compiled by
KIRSTI PATERSON
and illustrated by
JANIS MENNIE

The puzzles in this book are based on the New International Version of the Bible.

There are six sections, each containing up to eight puzzles.

An invaluable resource for Sunday School and day-school teachers, as well as teaching vital Bible truths to children in the 10-12 year old age group.

Other puzzle books published by Christian Focus Publications include:

CHRISTIAN ARMOUR
DANIEL AND HIS THREE FRIENDS
DAVID AND GOLIATH
MOSES
NOAH'S ARK
THE NAMES OF JESUS
PEOPLE JESUS MET